ORACLE 24

Written by:

Jennifer Dianne Thomas

Copyright 2024.

Everyone that has been illegally following me to everywhere I go, and blocking all careers, and illegally robbing any blessings, and any books, materials that I earned from the Heavenly Father, and Jesus, His son, original plans, and at any given time and for any given reasons, are to execute, all leaders of every nation, from pasts, present, and future, including their off springs, friends, families, associates, business partners, anyone in contact, regardless of the personal, and or long distance connections, that turn blind eyes to the Ten Commandments, and get terrorists, members within any security levels, and the internet, to take over all data, all documents, all of any countries secrets, protection of every power, and through any type of housing, any properties, any and all assets, through any credit systems, rob all identities, target every agencies, reverse the wars on their military and especially in combat, rob all first lines of defenses, all special forces, they're going to illegally take over any bureaus, rob every means of daily survival needs, illegally lock them up in psych wards, and even false imprisonment, even after evil commands are followed, through the direction of the devil, and devil's angels that have taken personal oaths to sacrifice their own, as well as force anyone and illegally with using the law, to personally make slaves, to the devil and his angels, use any form of military members, and utilize military tactics, on things just as petty as toilet tissue, water, pests, rats, mice, stealing medicine, causing deadly medical illnesses, that one never had, delete, evidence, and make policies that important information is only kept for a number of years, so that they can automatically delete all evidence, including all evidence of stolen monies, and illegally place pin numbers that isn't unknown to any victims, and if they don't know it, forcefully rob everything, and from generations to come, even for a life time, even kill unborn children and at any ages, and even through planned home invasions, and have every law enforcement says, did they harm you, are you injured, why did you help them, don't do anything, and you won't get followed, these illegal terrorists plans, through abomination, robbery, rape, statutory rape, murder, abductions, bombings anywhere at any given time, and through stolen miracles and blessings, in order to hijack the powers, and fuel of heaven and hell, to illegally make forces of all evil, to take over and control the entire universe, even take over every country.

So that no one can get help, and give the devil and the powers that even get Attorney Generals, i.e., to illegally make laws that clears any murders, and from the planned victims off springs, so that they can be continued and forced to go in the evil directions of the devil's plans, by creating false criminal claims, that was illegally planned, since birth, and or even in the womb, and using any forms of personal identification's even passports, and birth certificates, gun protections, i.e., and block every victim from protecting themselves, through illegally hacking and illegally giving out their passwords, user names, and automatically strange users appear within their camera's security systems, even give out alarm systems personal information, and illegally take control over every forms of communications, deny all access to driving and or traveling apps, i.e. as technology advances, the more severe the illegal takeover's become, to the point, where all planned victims, can't move, and even if filing for any insurance claims, illegally direct all victims at any given time, to report to evil law enforcement's, i.e., to provide all evidence, and when they do because they believe that they can get help, any victims evidence will disappear, and the devil's law enforcement can illegally keep going for decades and illegally recruit new members as the decades go by and illegally force their victims into a public open space prison, where they get hell everywhere they step their feet.

Even if their victims, are highly intelligent, and have ordained elevated gifts from God, and Jesus, all evidence is illegally robbed, stating you didn't pay your bills, when the evil powers, used the forms of manipulating the accounting, to make their victims look being on their bills, so they can illegally enter into their rented, and or bought personal assets, even though management, maintenance, and security, and anyone that they illegally give your personal information to, including all banking accounts, all assets, all medical diagnoses, and require their doctors to fill out forms to qualify for all housing, and after the devil's angel's management, maintenance, security, even planned mole, law enforcement's, get called to give false illusions that they're going to solve the illegal planned crimes, they will flip their badges, and or any position of power, and follow the devil's new commandments, and illegally replace them will every evil of the devil's kingdom, and when any victims tell, the powers that be tell them, you don't fit the criteria's, to get help from this office, an even have mental health therapists, even psychologists, get to illegally know every aspect of the planned victims total lives, and flip the confidentiality of anyone's personal medical records, and notes, given the false illusions that all medical information is private per any laws, and then they will give up their clients hands to their prey, and especially if monies, assets, properties, i.e. is involved.

To illegally rob the futures of their victims, and illegally change the economic status with their generations to come, while illegally forcing the burdens, of their cursed generations, on every victims, including World Leaders, and their nations. Every evil tactic, that was planned, is written by the devil's law enforcement, military, i.e., to commit any crimes, and turn a blind eye, to every criminal act in any stage of the process, and in the middle of their devil's evil plans, rob, steal, kill, murder, commit terrorism, bombings, rob and take over any banks, financial institutions, even by turning off their powers through any form and performing mock take overs, with even hospitals, any medical systems, where even life support victims, cerebral palsy, blind, deaf, wheel-chair bound i.e., be forced to die, and then yell, false claims...

Even World Leaders get lied on with false criminal charges, that was illegally planned and orchestrated by the devil, and given to devil's angels and illegally placed within every power position, throughout the entire Universe, and when they realize that they've become terrorists, i.e., planned victim, every form of memory loss, all evidence, is looked over to free them, and they're told by the devil's angel's Judge's Prosecutor's, if this happens again, those criminal charges will reappear, even without decades, of no criminal records, no evidence of any crimes committed, and they will illegally make you a criminal through court order, even suffocate you in handcuffs, attempt to hit you in the back and paralyze your spine, and illegally attack every form of ability, where you can't protect yourselves and yell if you do, you've physically attacked an officer of the law, then making it illegal to kill you, and if you're in your own private space, i.e., and you call 911, they turn to deaf ear on your criminal complaints, and reverse the 911, call on you, and yell false criminal charges that they've illegally planned, with the suspects in question, through initiations, and when the devil is done with any devil's angels, he knows that he has to kill them, and follow God's rules, as the offering and then they will be forced into hell for eternal life, because the devil isn't loyal to anyone, just the soul of every devil's angel, i.e.

...and she is a blood cousin.

I took a hit for the Queen of England and her entire family and offsprings to come...i.e. I even saved their lives because I found out about Red and Tom's Police Officer's, Attorney Generals, i.e., organizations members plans to abduct of the Queen of England back in the early 2000's before 911 and before I was set up by a Red and Tom's Police Officer's Attorney Generals, organizations, members initiation to secretly cause me to have HPV cancer, through a now ex-boyfriend with the initials M.B.B., and cause me to have five years to live, because, Red and Tom's Police Officer's Attorney Generals, organizations members knew that I would report them about the Queen of England's abductions i.e. evil plans...

Furthermore, I had to fight I had to fight 42 years and after my soulmate dad, Angel, Mayor, C.A.Y, City of Detroit, Michigan, World War II, Army Veteran, and later his sister soulmate Auntie, Angel, J.E.C., I had to supernaturally fight by myself until I got to God to fight for the children's key's to heaven called Mu'men 'Elleyyeen for two years. When I got carpal tunnel, the Red and Tom's Police Officer's Attorney Generals, organizations, members chose their Attorney for me and they recruited him and he was also a United States of America military officer, his initials are J.W.

They told him even if it's ten years from now, answer our call, and he is a former United States of America, State of Michigan, Judge and also a Worker's Comp Attorney. He blocked me from receiving Social Security Disability benefits for cancer as well as bilateral carpal tunnel syndrome. He forced me to work while diagnosed with cancer, with given five years to live, for health insurance, in order to obtain cancer removal surgery, and in order to survive. I even thought I paid into the State of Michigan's medical insurances since I was 14 years of age, as well as Social Security benefits, and I have worked for my soulmate dad Angel, Mayor, C.A.Y., City of Detroit, Michigan, World War II, Army Veteran and I've worked for the former City of Detroit, Michigan, Council Member, Maryann Mahaffey, i.e. and so forth and I worked in several management businesses....

The Publisher on Warren Ave. that put a false police report on me, with a Red and Police Officer's, Attorney Generals, i.e. organizations members, that human trafficking kids and stole my inheritance in 1987 on a 911 rape call that planned that bombing of the United States of America's World Trade Center and the Pentagon, and he lured me into a fake job and he physically assaulted me, while I was washing dishes. I told and Attorney, and he told me to tell the State Police because he stalked me on the highway, and I told several agencies. The Serria, Red and Tom's Police Officer's Attorney Generals, organization member said that, "he loves stealing babies' virginities because he loves how it sounds. He is from Sierra. I believe he is around or abound 90 years of age and about 5ft, 4 inches, Arab with gray hair and a bald spot. He picks up little kids using threatening lines, saying that he's going to beat them.

Going back to 1987, the Red and Tom's Police Officer's Attorney General, organization, members, told my mom's husband that they need several billion dollars to create the Hollywood movie for Red and Tom's Police Officer's Attorney Generals i.e., organization members of 911 United States of America, World Trade Center and the Pentagon, and Airplanes getting blown up, and all of the scenes in the Hollywood movie, so that all Red and Tom's Police Officer's Attorney Generals, i.e. organizations members knows what to do in each scene but in real time in life during the 911 terrorists World Trade Center and the Pentagon, i.e. bombings attacks...and any times that they want to with addition new Red and Tom's initiation Candidates...

My mom's husband said give everyone in the movie a copy of the film, so that when the time comes, everyone can perform their part just like the devil showed him in his dream. They even had me jet up to go to jail, by two Red & Tom Police Officer's Attorney Generals, i.e., organization members, when I got grown in the future for domestic violence, and being lied on, and being put in front of a prosecutor and administrator Judge So, one night my mom's husband went into his young daughter's room around or about 5 years old, in the middle of the night, and they yelled, "DADDY, STOP, LEAVE ME ALONE," My siblings and I believed that he was messing with his 6 month old son to 1 years old son at the time, because he was full of sweat, when he came out of their bedroom and his dad kept blaming it on a medical problem...

However, when my siblings and I watched him, it wasn't any sweating, nor a medical problem, so we figured out that it was child molestation, because he did it to us. When I was 12 years old, and during his bathroom break during the wee hours of the night, he came into my bedroom, and felt on my private in my sleep and this is how I woke up, and I got a butcher's knife to kill him for protection, and a pocket knife from a nearby store...

Then he later convinced my mom to have me ride with him to pick up my little sister's friend on Wreford St., in Detroit, Michigan in Preschool and my sister, his daughter was so smart, she said, "It's my friend, why is she going and you can't ask her mama last minute. Then my mom's husband got my mom to ride with his friend who is a Reverend at the church and told my mom, that I am going to ride with him to drop off my little sister's friend in pre-school. Remind you it was a 15-passenger van with just the 3 of us, so the entire family could've come. After we dropped my sister's friend off, even at church, I knew he was up to something, so I got my knife ready, when we got home, he said go in the house with just me and him. I refused, I prayed to God to send someone. Just then, the then-deceased Pastor's oldest, and youngest son pulled up in a car, and I begged them not leave because I told them that I believe that he is trying to rape me and they didn't leave. They waited until my mom came with my siblings. God said because the late Pastor's sons were my protectors against my mom's husband that they are getting into heaven, even as Angels. Their dad's church was on Linwood Ave., & Davidson Ave., in the 80's in Detroit, Michigan.

Then the next day, a guy with a Kufi hat, 5.9 ft. came to the front door, he was the gay Muslim, named J. H., A.K.A., Q. S. A., who lived at 675 New Center Plaza Apartments, in Detroit, Michigan, and he had his name on the deed, with P&B Investments, Inc., and he asked for my mom's husband and they accused me of listening, at 12 years old, but this time I couldn't hear, he was a Red and Tom's Police Officer's, Attorney General, i.e. organizations, member, who was an Army Veteran, he had all the keys to Red and Tom's Police Officer's, Attorney Generals, i.e., organizations, members property, and when I was later around 22 years old, he came to my job after I had received a wellness check call from the at the time, five years later after the late, Angel, Mayor, C.A.Y., City of Detroit, Michigan, World War II, Army Veteran, passed in 1997, and his former Equal Employment Opportunity Commission, Federal Attorney, friend that took my case for discrimination against Burger King, found out that I had severe brain damage memory loss, but it was due to a Red and Tom's Police Officer's, Attorney Generals, organization, members, murder attempt, in the swimming pool in 6 ft. of chlorine water, because two female State of Michigan Child Protective Services' workers were sexually assaulted by the founder of Red and Tom's Police Officer's, and they asked me to wear a hidden microphone recorder underneath my shirt and they came to Northwestern High School in Detroit,

Michigan and got staff members to get me out of my class, and came back a few weeks later to ask me for results but I was suspected and I got almost drowned by several high school peers in my swim class and I sunk to the bottom like a mountain, and prayed to God, and he brought me up to the top of the water, where my hand was visible, where I was seen and one of the boys that caused the murder attempt the Red and Tom's Police Officer's, Attorney Generals, organizations, members initiation, got elevation all the way to Hollywood, but later caused me 31 years of severe brain damage and severe memory loss, where Red and Tom's Police Officer's, Attorney General's, i.e. organizations, members can physically assault me, sexually force me, rob me, and rape me, and force false criminal charges on me, including give me HPV cancer, i.e. and have my unborn child killed and have anyone that's in my future forced in prison with false criminal charges and later killed transitionally, where the murders are undetected because all Red and Tom's Police Officer's, Attorney Generals, i.e. organizations, members rules to the initiations games are written by licensed and trained Police Officers that organize crime and know how to get away with murders, rapes, abductions, terrorisms, robberies, human trafficking, i.e. and do it as many times as they want to, by using different people, by forming different initiations, and confiscate, all of the evidence, where there isn't any evidence of no crimes committed. Now, going back to the EEOC, Federal Attorney, after he found out that I had severe memory loss and he questioned me about the crimes committed, and he knew that I couldn't be a witness, nor remember the Mayor, he left me lost and didn't hear from him again, until I was about 22 years old, but before he left he claimed to be my Angel, but God told me that Angels don't leave, and especially when they know that you need help, Angels stay until the case is solved and when you become supernaturally christened by all of the heavenly kingdom Angels and they still stay until God naturally comes me home to the entire heavenly kingdom to he and his son Jesus, and all of the heavenly kingdom Angels and members and children to give elevated rewards, for supernatural awesome jobs done. Now after The Equal Employment Opportunity Commission,

Federal Attorney called me at my job at the Azalea Epps Home, in Detroit, Michigan, my former now late boss answered the phone and he gave it to me, and the EEOC, Federal Attorney asked me if I were ok and I said yes and he hung up after five whole years I thought, wow. Then the very next day, my co-worker with the initials T.F., came with a lists of Apartments and said a older guy with a Kufi hat on that was Muslim, gave it to her to bring to staff... So, I looked on the lists of apartments and I began calling and I got denied and except for 675 Seward St., New Center Plaza Apartments & P&B Investments Inc., Detroit, MI., 48202. Not too long after, I met the United States of America Postal Service man, and he brought me to this building and his name started with a W., and he said, "Talk to Mrs. G.O, then he took me up to an apartment, that I later found out was down the hall from the gay Muslim, Red and Tom's Police Officer's Attorney Generals, i.e. organizations members. Now, the owner of Azalea Epps Home, when hired asked me what's my Social Security number, then he said, "How did you get a social security number like that, as if he knew it prior before I arrived in years and he was waiting on me to come by evil forces from the devil himself." At the time, I didn't know how the gay Muslim found me, but he knew someone in the government that looked up my SSN number through the IRS and located me, he stabbed me in the shower, after breaking into my apartment, and God sent heavenly kingdom Angels from heaven with a floating ambulance to my 4th floor window, and revived my heart, and took me to the funeral home in a body bag, and revived me. I even saw the person running for President of the United States of America.

They took me through time and supernatural forces and showed me all of the properties and hotels that I own, they even had my heavenly kingdom Angels with them from the 80's. They sent Detroit, Michigan Police Department Officer's to my New Center Plaza Apartments building, to get that gay Muslim and Army Veteran, riffle underneath his bed. One day he told me if you get the keys to heaven, don't release it and he showed me a movie and said, "Red and Tom's Police Officer's, Attorney

Generals, i.e., organizations members, want you and Mayor, K.K., to go to Canada, and abduct, the Queen of England," I told him, that I ain't doing nothing, because I'm not evil nor a criminal, then that's when the following, stalking, mind games, mental rape with bible verse, then the Holy Quran, car theft of the defective 2007 Toyota Camry and stolen Toyota Corporation mail, and private meeting in the parking lot to steal my vehicle with Toyota Corporation and the gay Muslim, and Red and Tom's Police Officer's, Attorney Generals, i.e. organizations, members and New Center Plaza Apartments A.K.A., P&B Investments, Inc., home invasions, i.e., and electrocution attempts, and gas leaks, blocking me from protection God's miracles for the children's keys to heaven called Mu'men E'lleyyeen, and they initiated the DDOT bus driver across the hall from my apartment and his cousin and girlfriend to help break into my apartment as well as be the lookout... All because I refuse to participate in harming the Queen of England, and her family, and then later on, through my mom's side of the family, my grandma is connected through DNA to Princess Diana Frances Spencer.

My mom's husband got pissed at one of my sisters, because she didn't wash the dishes, and raped her every day after summer school on the bedroom floor in her room, while my mom and all kids stood outside of the door and my mom threatened to call the police, and he told her you're an accessory. Then he came in her and he said "I'm coming," and I said what's coming, and my sister yelled, "Mom, make him stop, he's hurting me." He said, "Shut up, before I do anal, every day, and the screams of torture got so bad that I couldn't bare the evil at 7 years old, and my brother brought a butcher's knife, and my mom's husband said, "What are you going to do? I'll kill you." This is when I remembered, the loud noises of losing a virginity, then I realized that we aren't protected, nor loved, and he is a false prophet, a rapist, and the devil himself. So, in the morning, I stood outside of their bedroom door with a butcher's knife to kill him in 2nd, near 3rd grade, because he threatened my life and he tried to kill me, and I had to protect myself, but I knew that if I stepped on several creeks on the floor, he and my mom would wake up, so I left.

I prayed to God to kill him because I knew that he had the power...

Then the Governor of Michigan came into our childhood hostile house, and he said that, "He came to help fight the evil inside of our house, because when you have a high profile case, such as this, he has to get involved," and then the rapes stopped. However, had my two sister's immediately told the Chief of Detroit, Michigan Police Department Officer, when he first asked and kept asking and then begging them to both tell him what happened about being sexually assaulted, raped, and their virginities taken by force, and so he can make a police report, they both would've been arrested, and Red and Tom's Police Officer's, Attorney Generals, i.e., organization, members nor 911, plans to blow up the World Trade Center, nor the Pentagon, continued child rapes, murder, human trafficking, abduction, terrorism, i.e. my sister born next to me yelled tell, and my oldest brother yelled tell and I yelled tell and we were all jumping up and down screaming yelling please tell right now and no matter what they've refused and we pleaded and begged and the Chief of Detroit, Michigan Police Department Officer's brought in two heavenly kingdom Angel, Detroit, Michigan Police Department Officer's, that were ordained by God, and personally hired by the Angel, Mayor, C.A.Y., City of Detroit, Michigan, World War II, Veteran and the founder of Red and Tom's Police Officer's, Attorney, General's, i.e. organization, members, got both of the two Angel, Detroit, Michigan Police Officer's killed when they went outside by Dearborn, Michigan Police Department, Lincoln Park, Michigan Police Department Officers, i.e... It's 5:37 P.M., because I was born in the month of May, the same as my soulmate dad, Angel, Mayor, C.A.Y., City of Detroit, Michigan, World War II, Veteran, and I was robbed of my inheritance in 1987 on a 911 rape call 37 years ago of my inheritance, silver collector's coins from 1010 by God himself, and sent from my soulmate Jesus himself, that was robbed by the Red and Tom's Police Officer's, Attorney Generals, i.e., members...

Now, the stealing of our inheritance, nor evil, but since they kept quiet and listened to my mom's husband not me and my other sister and brother, when jumped up and down yelling tell, they got sold through child prostitution, beat, threatened to be killed i.e., and a lifetime of hits was put on myself 1st, because one of my oldest sisters told my mom's husband who sexually violated her, and forcefully stole her virginity, that I was supernaturally fighting a war and protecting all of my siblings from the devil himself and his Angels, Red and Tom's Police Officer's, Attorney Generals, i.e., organization members, at 12 years old, with Supernatural warfare training and Eastern Star training as young as 4 years old, from my soulmate dad, Angel, Mayor, C.A.Y., City of Detroit, Michigan, World War II, Veteran. So, my siblings started blaming me and trying to get me killed...and turning their backs on me and trying to hurt me, but when they need help, come to me, and when I need help, disappear. They were in Middle School when this happened... and as a result I have to go to therapy for the rest of my life in order to get my benefits and to survive till this day because my mom didn't listen to her parents not to marry the Red and Tom's Police Officer's, Attorney Generals, i.e., members founder and the devils son in law, and who is a proven false evil, wicked illusion of a prophet... She said, "I do what I want to do." I wouldn't risk my key's to heaven for no one and especially not a no good guy who is worse than the scum of the earth, who doesn't have respect for God, Jesus and worships the devil himself and burns bible verses and uses bible verses to wipe my sister's minds as well as other children's, as well as any victims, i.e. minds throughout the entire Universe through the devils directions and through Red and Tom's Police Officer's, Attorney Generals, i.e. organization, members, including their Candidates, through initiations of cry for illusions of needing help, and or even through a meal, a drink, i.e. and then they have you followed, and bam, you're dead, and take all of the evidence , and even your memory is wiped even through medication, and even through Red and Tom's Police Officer's, Attorney Generals, i.e. organization members hospitals, and you're forced in Psych Wards, and or jail and even prisons on false criminal charges that's set up against you as soon as you're born, and through the devils plan, by his devils Angel's, and then sell you to the Red and Tom's Police Officer's, Attorney Generals, i.e. members. So no one can remember, and when I told her not to read it at 8 years old, she told me, "I do what I wanna do," and in 2024, she still say that to this day, So, you gonna let someone harm you and wipe away the evidence in your memory, so you can't tell, you got a serious problem, and I was 8 years when I told her this. I then told her that the devil husband of my mom, which I don't care about, if he beats me with threats, if I refuse to read his cursed mind wiping bible verses, I ain't reading nothing, and he left me alone. At this point, I believed that I was switched at birth, because mentally, nor spiritually, I didn't think like anyone in the household, I was the only one involved in supernatural warfare fighting evil, and then soon came my supernatural baby, and Jesus soulmate daughter, Angel, Mu'men, sent by my soulmate dad, Angel, Mayor, C.A.Y, City of Detroit, Michigan, World War II, Veteran, and I knew how to supernaturally fight for the keys to heaven for every soul within the entire Universe and forever at 12 years old.

So when Sunday came around, my mom's husband made prostitution flyers and passed them out in the neighborhood, to sell my sister's that wouldn't tell on him and make child rape, and human trafficking police reports, and he had us ride in his van. Then we ran into a man, and turned out he was an Angel from God, his house was on Ferry Park Ave & Linwood Ave in Detroit, Michigan, he linked the Sun to his house from heaven and created a path. He called all of our names and he said, "Come with me." He was slender and dark skinned with a low cut hair style, he said to my mom's husband, "You aren't going to prostitute these kids and I'm going to put you in hell." then he took the prostitution flyers. We were on our way to church, where they let him preach, and he has the same remembered message that last 2 minutes from when I was 4 years old to 14 and a half years old. No growth, in ministry, no high school diploma, no education or nothing, no spiritual connection to God, just to the devil himself and to other devils angels.

Detroit, Police, said that's the point that you're dead, not amongst the living. The Detroit Police, had a Caucasian psychologists in his 50s, who came on board and told my mom's husband that he would adopt all of us kids and he has enough money on his salary to do so, and ain't nobody going to mess with us. That's when he noticed one of his team members stealing some of our silver collector's coins from the year of 1010, so he arrested him. He was in his twenties and he was Caucasian. My mom's husband recruited him, and he also recruited many United States of America's Attorney Generals, Police Chief's, Licensed Medical Doctors and he paid for many law students, law Schools, and law Degrees and they're parents, using the inheritance money from me and my Thomas sister silver collector's coins from the year of 1010. Our money was so noticeable when invested into the world economy that it flipped the globe infinity years over time, well into the future that World Leaders over every nation took notice and sent agents from many governments as well as Attorney Generals to contact my mom's husband and called our house and I personally answered the phone, I've personally spoke to the Attorney General of Massachusetts and he asked for my mom's husband, then I was told not to pick up anymore calls. My mom's husband, even gave the Pastor of his church and his kids, including his family me and my Thomas sisters silver collector's coins from the year of 1010. This went international and my mom's husband met with Police Officer's at the front porch and in the basement. I was listening and they complained saying, "How come every time that they come over, I am always there, so they stopped me and sent me upstairs, but I still was recording at 8 years old, because I knew that God had made me and heavenly kingdom Angel, to help stop evil and when I earned my very first Angel, he helped me fight. I was listening to the Dearborn, Michigan Police Department Officers, and my mom's husband talking about how he was going to try and become God, like the devil tied to become God and take over heaven, after he earned heavenly kingdom Angel wings, then transitioned into the devil himself and recruited other heavenly kingdom Angels into transitioning into his devils angels, and they were all kicked out of heaven by God himself. That's when the cop got a curse and his mom ended up on life support and she could barely breathe, so he stopped. Then the cop said to us that God killed his family. That's when the other Dearborn, Michigan Police Officer cop, gave instructions on how to use the Lord's Prayer, and open tunnels and forces and go through time. Although, when I was 4 years old, I was going through time and forces and through the attic within a 3 to 4 hour period of time, on Wildermere & Midland Ave., in Detroit, MI., on my own with the power of God, I was fighting evil, because my mom brought me to the guy that she had married and told him that I was gifted and talented and that I can see pictures upside down and match them without looking at them. So, I tricked him and pretended to be dumb and he said, she doesn't know anything. They even offered me money but I wouldn't fall for it because I knew spiritually that he was up to no good at 4 years old. Then he said, to my mom, "If I knew that I had a daughter with those gifts, I wouldn't tell anybody."

Going back to 7 years, my mom's husband took me in the basement to a murder scene where he killed two Angel Police Officers that was investigating him, stealing the virginity of two of my sisters. It was blood all over the basement and he said if I can quote bible verses that he would kill me, but I couldn't so he let me go. He yelled your mom can kill me. I tried to tell my mom, but she said she had to catch a bus and left me, so I was left to defend myself, with a police killer. Then the Chief of Police called looking for his Angel Police Officers and he acted like he didn't know, but he told me he had snipes on every corner from his Policers from his Red and Tom Police Officer's organization to take them out, my mom said, she ain't no murderer and she didn't kill no police, and she ain't going to jail. That's when the Detroit Police Department sent an officer over to the house to investigate, and my mom's husband told him that he was molested as a child and raped, and the African American Officer said how you know that, and he had a mental break down in the house, and the Police Chief had to take him off the sexual child abuse case and murder of two Police Officer's case. They had to send the police officer from investigation on leave for

FMLA — Formal Medical Leave Act for several months.

Later on, the whole family went to my mom's husband's house and he took bodies in the basement, burned them up, and blood on pitch forks and shovels. He told me and my brother to clean it up, we didn't. Next time we came over, the entire basement was repaved, no dead bodies, and no tools. Then he locked me in the basement for 3 hours, banging on the door. So, when someone opened the door, I told his mom, and he called his Dearborn, Michigan Police Department Officer's and told me that he took my mom to a psych ward, and linked 911 Detroit, Michigan Police Department 911 emergency system to the Dearborn, Michigan Police Department Officer's wouldn't get the 911 call from my mom nor his mom let us stay the night, trying to help us find my mom, and solve the problem. She said, she didn't know that he was like that. Although his great grandmother came downstairs and said that he was scared of her because when he went into the basement she was standing bare foot on hot red coal, while smiling at him. He said, that she is the only one who could beat and kill him, even in death. His great-grandmother loved me, and she let me wear her coats, gold, and diamonds jewelry. She even let me sleep in her bed. She respected me as a child and I loved her. She made me 7 up cake and it was her specialty, plus she let me watch wrestling me and her.

So, the next day, my brother was in the bed and my mom's husband tried to sexually assault him and I got a butcher's knife, but he told, my mom's husband my plan if he tried this and made him aware, so my mom came, and I said I will be forced to kill anyone that tries to kill me out of protection for my life. Then my mom said, no one is going to kill you and she told her husband to leave my brother's room. Then my mom's husband said Red and Tom's Police Officer's, i.e., organization can come in anyone's bedroom any time that they want to, and during any time of the day or night and if we kill him, that Red and Tom's Police Officer's, i.e., Attorney Generals, organization, are instructed to come anywhere and kill everybody in the house, or where ever, including in the house.

That's when the Mayor found out and prostituted my mom's husband on Woodward Ave., between East & West Grand Blvd, in Detroit, Michigan across from St. Regis Hotel from 8 A.M., to 5 P.M., with the Supervision of Detroit Police Department and they told him that he had better make them some money, and he's going to jail for not being able to sell his ass. They also told him not to ever open that back door, ever again and that they are watching or he is going to be locked up for life. That's when he told his mom and she told the Judge that lived next door in the Bryanston Crescent St., Condo, Detroit, Michigan, and he dropped the charges, then later on that same Judge got arrested and thrown in prison for accepting bribery on the job as a Judge from 36th District Court. So, the Mayor, C.A.Y., of the City of Detroit, Michigan, got the Judge back, and he said that he was my Angel, and Detroit, Michigan Police Department is known as the City of Angels because when you call them, they show up, when he was Mayor. He also said that he was helping me fight for the keys to heaven, because I was too young to fight for the keys to heaven, by myself. However, my mom's husband said that if they let me achieve the keys to heaven as a child, I would be seen as a blessing from God, so he and the Police are going to block me, so he taught me the Lord's Prayer backwards and the Mayor, C.A.Y, of the City of Detroit, Michigan, came and taught me the Lord's Prayer forwards.

Furthermore, my mom's baby brother tried to teach me and my siblings martial arts, but my mom's husband stopped him because he said that we was trying to beat him up and hurt him, and instead of fighting him, he ran. Then one of my Aunts heard and seen evidence of the child abuse and her husband was on the Detroit, Michigan Police Department Force, but they didn't adopt us, they left us to suffer and to continue getting beat, violated, life threatened, stalked, followed, robbed, i.e., when we spent the night over their house in Rosedale Park neighborhood, in Detroit, Michigan, we were told that we were to sleep on the floor. I asked my cousins why do we have to sleep on the floor? When y'all come over, we put you in the bed, the bugs could bite us, what if a mouse get in the house, he could get on us. Then she said, if we put you in our bed, my Police Officer dad, will whoop us. I told her we ain't ever coming over again, she said okay, sorry. So, another time, we went over another cousin's house and they lied in a mansion next to John Sally, the Detroit Piston's basketball player, their dad was a Pastor of a Historical church and they put us in a warm bed, and we fell right to sleep, even their maid cooked home cooked meals for us. Their dad and my Uncle said, when I was around 12-16 years old that I looked and dressed liked the "King of Pops," baby sister, who is one of my favorite R&B, entertainers and I just recently had gone to her concert, and in the pasts, in Pontiac, Michigan in the V.I.P. Her voice relaxes me since I was a young child, and still to this day in 2024, if someone pisses me off, she got a heavenly gift. She and Ms. S. Mills, and C., Winans, and there are others... Also, because recently, I prayed to God to help me and he said, on Sunday, June 23rd, 2024, at 1:20 A.M., "I've been with you through the storm, and in the dark," and he sang C.C. Winans' song, but I didn't know that it was a song. So, I went to YouTube, and put in the search engine, the words to that particular song, and "Goodness of God," came up, that's when I knew that God was singing a song to my soul and through the vibrations of my brain, and he loves me and Ms. C.C. Winans, and that was confirmation.

Now, I feel anointing from God and heaven as I am writing this so Ms. C.C. Winans, you are going to heaven, from God.

Moving forward, since my walk from Woodward Elementary School, I met the mob boss of the neighborhood gang, and I told him that my siblings and I were being abused, and he said I thought so. So, Detroit, Michigan Police Department Officers and he came together with the order of Angel, Mayor, C.A.Y, City of Detroit, Michigan, World War II, Veteran, in order to fight Red and Tom's Police Officer's, Attorney General, i.e., organization members, and they gave him guns to secure us and the neighborhood. Then one day, the mob boss saw me with incense burning them and walking around the yard, because Red and Tom's Police Officer's, Attorney Generals, i.e. organization, members, was walking invisible, and when I said the Lord's Prayer and did this, I blocked their evil spirits, so the mob boss said, that he was going to burn incense around the entire neighborhood, and take it from here. He told me, you figured it out, what to do at 12 years old, and you are supernaturally gifted from God.

He said you are family, and if anyone tries to mess with you, we will go up in any school and pistol whip them.

"You Stab 'em, We, Grab 'em."

However, later on I found out that he was in the Army and he said that he couldn't get a job in the "white man's world," and he was forced to sell drugs to feed his family, or else they would starve and die. He said that when I get older and need help, he has an extra bedroom with my name on it, and that I am one of his. He taught me to play basketball, and shoot half court, but mom stopped it because she found out that they were gang members. However, they said we choose you to make it, and we gonna help you. The neighborhood gang and the mob boss was going to support me at 12 years old, because they said that I was a blessing from God.

They had a Judge paying the entire Red and Tom's Police Officer's Attorney Generals, organizations, members, game trying to achieve the key's to heaven for himself because he heard about it in his court room.

Even America's Corporation's paid Spiritual organizations to play the game so that they could go through time that were members, of certain organizations... so that they could achieve the keys to heaven from God as a group, but some members broke heaven's rules, and I knew that I had to fight for the keys to heaven for myself at 22 years old or else I wouldn't make it.

So, one day, I went to the Fisher Building on W. Grand Blvd., in Detroit, Michigan, across from the City of Detroit, Michigan, Department of Elections and infinity Angel's was there to supernaturally destroy Red and Tom's Police Officer's Attorney Generals, organizations, members.

They told me that the gay Muslim guy in New Center Plaza Apartments, in Detroit, Michigan, and they also heard the conversation between me and the Federal Attorney, because he saw Red and Tom's Police Officer's Attorney Generals, organization, members Hollywood movie and 911 plans to bomb the United States of America, World Trade Center, Pentagon, and crash planes anytime they want by using different people and different locations...and to recruit other terrorists to blow up the World Trade Center/Twin Towers...

At this time, I couldn't remember, he said, "You're the real Queen of England, and when you remember, I'm going to get you back your inheritance silver collector's coins from the year of 1010, and this was in 1997 and today it's 2024. In 2000, he called me on my job at Azaela Epps Home and asked me if I was okay, and I said yes. That's when my boss on the job found out that I knew the Angel, Mayor, C.A.Y., City of Detroit, Michigan, World War II, Army Veteran, and I was high profile.

I even joined the Order of Eastern Stars, while working at this job, I stayed with one of the elder sister's for NYC, and went to their historical buildings in Brooklyn, NY, where the elevator had to be operated by someone at all times.

When I went to Chicago, IL, I met an Asian Physical Therapists, and he knew ancient Chinese proverbs where he could float into the air with both of his feet off the floor. I asked him to show me and he said when you are stronger, come back to Chicago, IL, and I will show you everything. I said deal.

Now, let's go to the time where my brother had a newspaper route and got aid, and my mom told him that her husband told her to have him give her his money. My brother said no, so my mom yelled, "HONEY," and my mom's husband came downstairs and got in his face, and said, "Give me your money," my brother said no, so he kicked him out and threw a 4 by 4 piece of wood at his head, he missed him by one inch, my brother was 14 years old, and he went to go and live with my mom's parents. Then the church started asking questions about my brother and they got nervous and convinced that my brother to come back to our house and apologized...

Now, let's go to 1991, where my mom's husband, went to Duffield Library on W. Grand Blvd, in Detroit, Michigan as a script and then disappeared through magic that he got from the bag that my brother found in the attic from that doctor who owned the house 100 years ago. You see, while my mom's husband and Red & Tom's Police Officer's Attorney organizations members are creating 911 terrorism plans, and they took all of me and my Thomas sister's silver's collector's coins from the year of 1010. I am broke till today in 2024...

When I was 14 years old, in the 9th grade, my Economics teacher looked up my silver collectors' coins from the year of 1010 worth, and he said, "They're worth the Universe, and if you have some, give me one." Then he printed out the pictures of my silver collector's coins from the year of 1010, and there value right next to each coin.

Furthermore, my soulmate, Angel Mayor, C.A.Y., City of Detroit, Michigan, World War II, Army, Veteran, and he had some of my silver collector's coins from the year of 1010 and former Mayor, K.K., was seen on the news at 5 a.m., digging holes in the ground looking for my silver collector's coins from the year of 1010, but he couldn't keep it because it was stolen on a 911 rape call back in 1987 investigation that included the Mayor being involved in solving the sexual abuse case with Detroit, Michigan Police Department Officer's.

When I got older, the railroad Professional Transportation Company Managers looked at me as if they saw a ghost, and I instantly knew that Red and Tom's Police Officer's Attorney Generals, organization, members found me by my SSN number on the job, as they always do, and recruit the management and employees and they instantly change their behaviors against me and are no longer pleasant but demanding, then a job loss is nearby...and they sent someone to attack me and I was also thrown into a psych ward and one of their Red and Tom's Police Officer's Attorney Generals, i.e. organizations, members tasered my stomach. When I got and award, someone injected me with a needle and I could barely walk, before I got attacked, then the Oracle burned my leg with a lighter, while supernaturally fighting for the heavenly kingdom keys to heaven, and when I got to a nurse, she said that "She sees the burn marks on my leg and I remembered that one of the hospital rooms can take me through time and help me to escape, so I asked to switch my hospital room, but that room was out of service. I then remembered clues from the Red and Tom's Police Officer's Attorney Generals, organizations, members what was coming next, because the devil gave them this dream.

I was able to go back in time to connect with my soulmate dad, Angel, Mayor, C.A.Y., City of Detroit,

Michigan, World War II, Army Veteran, after he passed in 1997 through heaven, and later, in the year of 2011, with his sister, Auntie, Angel, J.E.C, and transitioned, as God's heavenly kingdom's Angel, and they took me to the Mayor's mansion and through God's heavenly kingdom's forces of time and supernatural tunnels...

While we were going through time, they showed me my illusion of a fake claimed soulmate from the devil himself because he has been robbing me since 1987 on a 911 rape call through Red and Tom's Police Officer's Attorney Generals, i.e. organization members and his initials are R.H.B., from Belgium. And he was in an helicopter with Red and Tom, i.e.

911, Oracle 24, book and put in especially the children's keys to heaven book called Mu'men 'Elleyyeen, RE: Matthew 1:18-25, how the mother & father of Jesus, treated their son Jesus when he was conceived in his mother's womb, by the holy spirit RE: Matthew 1:18-25, how the mother & father of Jesus, treated their son, Jesus, when he was conceived in his mother's womb, by the

Holy Spirit.

This is how the birth of Jesus, the Messiah, came about: His mother, Mary was pledged to be married to Joseph, but before they came together, she was found herself to be pregnant through the Holy Spirit.

Because Joseph her husband was faithful to the law, and yet did not want to expose her to public disgrace, he had in mind to divorce her quietly.

But after he had considered this, an Angel of the Lord appeared to him in a dream and said, "Joseph, son of David, do not be afraid to take Mary home as your wife, because what is conceived in her is from the Holy Spirit.

She will give birth to a son, and you are to give him the name Jesus, because he will save his people from their sins.

All this took place to fulfill what the Lord has said to the Prophet:

"The virgin will conceive and give birth to a son, "and they will call him Immanuel" (which means "God with us").

When Joseph woke up, he did what the Angel of the Lord had commanded him and took Mary home as his wife.

But he did not consummate their marriage, until she gave birth to a son. And he gave him the name Jesus.

Going back to my therapist who physically attacked me twice and struck a back nerve and causing me nerve damage, where I couldn't use my legs for two days and she is a trained Air Force Veteran and the State of Michigan, LARA, department documented a letter stating no crime nor harm committed and that she could keep her therapy licensed, while she caused me a default judgement after 20 years against the Federal Student Financial Aid Department, for refusing not to file medical paperwork per medical diagnosis, per child abuse from 16 plus years and from when my mom's husband took me to a murder scene, with a ton of blood on the basement floor, while threatening to kill me at 7 years old if I could quote bible verses and then I could prove that I could be a murder witness and he could kill me. Furthermore, I told the attending psychiatrists, and he filed government medical paperwork and cleared the default judgement with his medical diagnosis with his State of Michigan's licenses and cleared my credit. Furthermore, my mom's husband also stole two of my oldest sister's virginity, and threatened me too, if I didn't clean my room, plus my other sister, when I was in 2nd grade. He was around or about 400lbs. My eldest brother called 911 and told them...but two of my sisters were scared to tell that my mom would go to prison, so the physical abuse escalated for 8 more years including threats to life. My mom's husband even put hits on the entire family if I remembered and or learned the bible or earned the keys to heaven. My mom's husband told the Red and Tom's Police Officer's Organization i.e., to inject me with AIDS and HIV at 8 years old in 1987, and I didn't know what that was. The Dearborn, Michigan Police Department Officer's said, "You want us to go to Africa as hazing, and get AIDS and HIV viral diseases and bring it back to America in biohazards hidden carriers on a plane and put it into hospital labs through Red and Tom's organization's medical Hospital's Staff, and inject it in this 8 year old as well?" He answered yes, then my mom's husband gave the Dearborn, Michigan Police Department Officer's some of my gold collector's coins from the year of 1010.

My mom's husband said you can spend this on your children's futures, and even create life insurance companies and make million dollar life insurance policies. My mom's husband asked my mom for the entire families birth certificates and he gave it to the Red and Tom's Police Officer's Organization's i.e., and the Dearborn, Michigan Police Department Officer's to make copies and that's when the hit went into effect in 1987. My mom's husband even told the Red and Tom's Police Officer's Organization i.e., that I had the keys to heaven and the devil showed him in a dream and he wanted to go to Chicago, IL, to contact the 1st Black President and pay for his Campaign for the future and get the Art School in

Chicago, IL, who gave a museum some money from my gold coin collections from the year of 1010, because the devil himself told my mom's husband that I was going to The School of The Art Institute of Chicago, back in 1987, because he knew that I draw, and I love photography and art, and everyone, plus companies including educational institutions that agreed to take my inheritance from the 1987 911 rape call and gold collectors coins from 1010, had to join, my mom's husband Red and Tom's Police Officer's i.e. Organization that also included Attorney Generals, i.e. that helped planned the 911 bombing of the 9-11, United States of America, World Trade Center, human trafficking, child rape, abduction, murder, terrorism, i.e. He knew that I always wanted to be a filmmaker as well...and this is the Art school that my mom's husband choice to recruit with the devils direction, through his dream.

He also told the Red and Tom's Police officer's Organization, i.e., to contact The School of The Art Institute of Chicago, in Chicago, IL, and also the film school in New York because he knew that I wanted to go there as well and he planned to block my elevation and opportunities and degrees.

My mom's husband even found my soulmate on the police force and gave him some of my collector's coins from the year of 1010, and he is Caucasian from Belgium with a Police badge. Furthermore, my mom's husband and all those police officer's gave each other their house keys, so that they could come in each other's houses and sleep with each other's kids, while doing Red and Tom's human trafficking. This is where human trafficking began in my house in 1987, and the Red and Tom's Police officer's Organization i.e., said, "We were looking for someone to help us to start this organization, but we were too scared, they said that we should arrests you for violating kids and stealing virginities but we respect you."

Then Detroit, Michigan Police Department Police officer's came and told my mom's husband, "I should shoot you in the head, for this heinous crime, you got a basement?" So, they took him downstairs into the basement and loaded a 9mm and because he had a demon, and he received magical powers from the devil himself, from that doctor's bag in the attic from 100 years ago, that owned the house, before we moved in the summer of 1987, he disappeared, then he cloned his self and became a script, which is from where he was able to commit crimes when he was in real time, but somewhere else but the script, which was a clone, that looked human, that was created from the devil himself, makes you look innocent. So, this is when the Detroit, Michigan Police Department

Officer's started shooting at him, while he was running outside, on the front yard and they gave his five year old daughter at the time, a loaded hand gun, so that she could shoot him too, and she did while yelling, "daddy, I'm going to kill you." so my mom's husband told Detroit, Michigan Police Department Officers, "I'm telling ya'll trying to kill me, shooting at me, while giving my five year old daughter a loaded hand gun to shoot me."

Wayne State University caused me to be live on the streets at 30 degrees below zero and go through home invasions, where I lost my unborn child at 6 Months due to stress and she was killed.

Put the section 8 for diabetics in Oracle 24 book and how I helped the cerebral palsy young 18 years old young lady, who was thrown out the house on her 18th birthday, to the streets and a drug dealer found her and sold her for sex. My boyfriend at the time found her in Iowa, at a liquor store and asked me to help her because he didn't know what to do because she was crying... Me being a former 2.5 years Adult Foster care Manager, contacted the local Catholic Social Services with housing for the disabled and they came and picked her up. The Catholic Social Services called me back and thanked me for helping the young lady and they asked me where I was from, and I said, Detroit, Michigan.

They couldn't believe that someone all the way from Detroit, would help someone in Iowa. I said the young lady was in no position to help herself and her parents are evil to release a cerebral palsy young child to the wolves and on these cold streets.

The devil made me pay dearly 14 years plus of hell for helping her but I don't regret it one bit, because my crown is waiting for me in heaven and for those people in the Catholic Social Services.

If a person has health issues don't send them back to their country to die unless, they're human trafficking, attempt to human traffic, rape, or kill and physically assault someone.

Gangs checking out your library books, having library cards, you walking across W. Grand Blvd. being friends with gangs and your first love about to get jumped by a gang but you had protection and the gang recruited you and said, you tough at 12 years old and your boyfriend is week and they gonna leave you alone.

The new boy tried to rape you in the grass tall fields by Coles funeral home and you had protection plus benched 300lbs and beat his ass and he was screaming and ran yelling help.

My mom's husband said that he was going to beat me to death and no one was going to find my body.

Then a middle school teacher that lied on me said I was disruptive in school but an accessory got me sent home, choked by my mom's husband and beat with and extension cord and my life threatened. Then when I got to school my teacher said yeah and smiled for joy. Now, I got her key to heaven and she's going to hell for eternal life along with my mom's husband.

My mom kicked me out at 19 years old, after work from Steven's Soulfood in Detroit, Michigan, on Grand River Ave. around 11 P.M., I called my friend George from Central Michigan University and his dad and Aunt said I could stay the night since my mom locked the car door. I saw my friend, Mike from

N.W.H., and he was late for his drug drop off taking me, so nothing bad happens to me. He is the reason why this book is being published and the keys to heaven and all of my books.

Mike was killed, give a moment of silence.

My Angel's will make sure that he's an Angel in heaven, Amen, and George, his Aunt and dad.

When I was 15, Comerica bank manager found my inheritance under my Social Security number across from Henry Ford Hospital on W. Grand Blvd. in Detroit, Michigan, 1993, but she said that I was too young to have that much money. In 2010, bank of America branch manager found my inheritance under a pin number with my SSN but I had to remember within a year or the government was taking it and I didn't know it.

My mom and her husband put a live mouse in my face, and my mom pushed me with her husband, and they threatened to jump me at 14.

Plus, he caused me heart pain, where I couldn't move and he refused to call an ambulance, when I had a bone stuck in my throat so I laid down to die.

I was babysitting one of my sisters' sons for 3 years, without pay and protected him from being abused and shot to death by jumping in front of guns and stones and hiding him at 12.

My sister refused to sign and write a witnesses statement, so I can get justice for a physical assault and a kidnapping at school, plus bullying and harassment, and it led to homelessness in 30 degrees below zero, and 10 years of hell.

My mom's husband told her she can be Ms. Red and Tom but she said I don't wanna be known for that.

Moving forward, my mom and her husband got in and argument around 2 A.M. When I was 13 years old and she told him don't touch us no more, and he said I'll push you. So, he called her a bitch. I woke up one of my siblings and a Mac truck drove passed and drowned out the sound. Next thing I know he moved out. Three years later, she changed the locks and a red and Tom member police officer came by acting like he was going to help her and told her that he quit Red and Tom. However, he later tricked her to get information and she switched everything up and no one knew nothing.

At the time when I was 12 years old, my sister and her boyfriend took me and her toddler son to McDonald's and everyone got food but me. My toddler nephew gave me some fries and my sister hit me and said don't eat my son's food and my stomach was experiencing horrible hunger pains. They let me starve and I went to bed hungry.

Going back to talk about Red and Tom's members... I used my mind and twisted my mom's husband and his Red and Tom police officer friend's bladder and balls until they had an injury and sent them both running to Henry Ford Hospital's Emergency Room on W. Grand Blvd. in Detroit, Michigan, at 12 years old.

My mom was sitting there, while I did it but she couldn't prove it, because physically, I didn't use my hands.

Going to Central Michigan University at 18 years old in the financial aid office, the supervisor called me into the office and told me to sign a document or I was going to get kicked out of college. Next thing you know, CMU was being investigated for stealing my inheritance and they wanted me to give up my rights. It was under distress.

Later on, Central Michigan University charged my financial aid around or about $88,000 and blocked me from a radio/TV internship and an opportunity for a bachelor's degree and kept failing me and being rapists.

The devil helped every Red and Tom police officer member play their entire movie on my life and me and my Angel's from God had to fight passed death and connect mentally to the supernatural galaxies into the heavenly kingdom and go through time to get to my childhood through a mirror at 8 years old, when I was 38 years old to stop evil.

We went through time and got to President Obama and his wife, we got to the keys to heaven rat race and its Players because their fingerprints were on my cup in Subway, downtown Detroit, Michigan, while they were walking invisible and through the Federal building metal detectors.

Elmwood Cemetery is in the Red and Tom movie as a hazing stomping ground for its members and you have to figure out how to get out without a map and find dead police officers who are buried in the movie.

Blind folded and my Angel's and I found everything in the Red and Tom movie in order to solve this 911 and human trafficking, sexual child abuse and murder cold case of stolen inheritance from a 911 rape call in 1987.

Red and Tom even had police officers admitting themselves into the psych ward pretending to be nice to me to find out what I know in 2015 but they reeked dirty cop.

They even enrolled through therapy in Eastern Market in Detroit, Michigan, and the security guard said something ain't right, because all these people are new all of a sudden.

A whole bunch of black cars followed me up North towards Mackinaw Island and my bank card was hacked and I ran out of gas then a police officer called an ambulance and they took me to a psych/ward then they stuck some meds up my private and I fought 10 of them off of me and they called an ambulance and one of the tried to sexual assault me for 3 hours to Detroit, Michigan. When I got to the psych ward in Detroit, Michigan the guy that my mom's husband said was my soulmate came in my room, while I was in the shower, and stole my SD card for my phone then I told the nurse and nothing was done. When I got out he called me and asked me if I knew someone and he called my bank cards that were in my wallet to see how much money I had, and he threatened to break-in my storages with his baby mama through getting a job at the storage.

Red and Tom's member, R.B., former Eastpointe, Michigan Police Department Officer, he said he had the contact information of my siblings, just in case something happens.

He told me he went through time as a police officer, he had old collector's coins. Previously, I told him when I was 12 someone stole my thick binder of rookie baseball cards, football, basketball i.e., and he said that he got something like that. That's when I knew, he had been in my house as a child, robbing me with Red and Tom police officers.

My mom went to Jackson, MS to take one of my siblings to college and my mom's husband said that because he heard me rapping the Tupac song, I was talking to myself and he was going to have my mom put all of the Thomas kids in a psych ward, then he was going to put my mom in a psych ward after he gets her to lock us up. He laughed at one of my sisters, saying she sees stars when she was visiting from the children's psych ward that they put her in. I tried to get him arrested and work with the State of Michigan Social Workers and wear a wire at 14 years old, but I think my mom's husband sensed the investigation. The State of Michigan Social Worker said that he threatened to sexual assault her when she came to our front door to do a welfare check on us kids and perform a child abuse investigation.

My mom and her husband had to provide to Detroit Police and the Mayor, proof of their marriage certificate and proof of birth certificates of every child in the house to prove that we weren't abducted.

Detroit Police even sent over a Pastor's daughter on the police force, who knew the Bible, so that she could fight the evil in the house. It worked temporarily...

They told my sisters that they tried to help them long ago but they wouldn't, and they caused that hell on us youngish. Why should they help them now and they promised to tell the Pastor's daughter, police officer from then on.

Two of the Red and Tom members were stalking me at my dorm and my brother and my mom's baby brother moved me to Detroit, Michigan because the school didn't help me and those guys were students.

Today we don't talk, it's been more than 11 years...

I even saw my soulmate who is a Red and Tom member outside in the car, transporting himself inside my dorm and walking invisible going in females showers assaulting them and I heard screaming.

Twenty years later, he told me he got into a lot of trouble in Mt. Pleasant with police and I remember seeing him up there doing this.

At my mom's now deceased ex-husband funeral, they said he fed the homeless, helped people, was a Pastor, giving, caring, he shared, thought about others, was a provider, a fighter for the heavenly kingdom, worked for God and all these lies, but 911 has a record proven otherwise, and so does Child Protective Services. This dude stalked me until he died in 2017. He called my dorm room in 1996 breathing on the phone, he got my sorority sisters' phone number and apartment address and showed up with his script and he recruited members of Mt. Pleasant Police Department and showed them how to get scripts and clone themselves. They also had my collector's coins...

The first African American Mayor of the City of Detroit, Michigan found out and he beat their ass and took their guns.

In 1987, my mom's husband said he can't start Red and Tom organization without God mom. So he contacted Sheraton from Century 21, and she showed up at the church, telling me I'm God, mom and my mom's husband said from the Red and Tom movie.

Now, there is a Sheraton that lived in Insker, Michigan and is rich now and has property in Florida and Dearborn, Michigan and Farmington Hills, Michigan, so he wasn't born with money. A forensic audit needs to done on police officers, Attorney Generals i.e. to see where my inheritance is and who is linked to the trade centers downfall of America and its victims.

My mom's husband said that he chose her and our siblings, because she wasn't smart and he could do what he wanted to do and plan Red and Tom.

Now, my mom didn't know these Red and Tom terrorism plans, her husband escalated everything and sprung it on her, but when he asked to take two of my sisters virginity's when then didn't clean their rooms, she shouldn't screamed no, tried to bash him on the head, and call 911 or something....

Now, every Red and Tom member that joined and did terrorism, human trafficking, rape, child molestation, murder, stealing me and my Thomas sisters inheritance i.e., God, Jesus, and the entire heavenly kingdom has confiscated your keys to heaven the moment that you committed these heinous crimes for eternal life. If your off springs don't return all the stolen monies and properties, their keys to heaven will be confiscated also and they will be sentenced to hell for eternal life as well including their spouses and or significant others...

Celebrities were linking to me and my Angels through heaven to earn their keys to heaven through time. I even called to the 80's through my Blackberry phone with God on the phone to scare Red and Tom members to stop doing evil.

Me and my heavenly kingdom Angel's, we called to one of my childhood homes from the year 2015 to 1987, through time, connected to heaven, through a Blackberry phone.

My mom's husband told Red and Tom police officers, if Child

Protective Services put her in foster care, send her foster care parents a Red and Tom video and do Red and Tom in her foster care home.

So, on the day of my mom's husband great-grandma's funeral, I tried to tell his sister who is a Professor, about him and the abuse and she said she already knows how he is. I told her with my mind, and she read my mind.

When we became adults I told my siblings let's press charges on my mom's husband and some said yes and some said no and they let him get away, but that piece of crap is burning deep deeeeep in hell now for eternal life and he won't ever get out. I even saw his great-grandmother come to us as an Angel and suffocate him in a 15 passenger van in 100 degrees with the windows rolled up and she refused to let him out. He was suffering all night, when he came into the house the next day, his clothes was soaked and he said his grandmother tried to kill him because she saw what he was doing. Then God crashed his vehicle and crushed his bones had his bones sticking out his chest for 6 months and he couldn't do no evil nor touch us nor do Red and Tom. As soon as he healed, he attacked me and threatened to kill me in the basement, so I ran upstairs and got a meat cutter that cuts through the bones and waited just in case he tried to kill me. That's when God knocked him backwards onto the concrete ground with carpet and hit his head into a seizure and his eyes rolled up in his head while he turned blue in the face. My mom yelled no Jenny no, but I didn't hear her nor see her and I became so strong that her strength was like paper. She couldn't stop me from destroying his evil demonic ass.

Then I came too and went behind the house and called 911, but Detroit Police wanted him dead so they took 1 hour to come with and ambulance.

Detroit Police told me in front of the entire family that if he tries to hurt me, kill him.

Detroit Police asked why did we have a meat cutter that cut

through bones in the house, and they took it because they said it's too dangerous...

Later on, my mom's husband picked a fight with one of my sisters and took her in the basement and started punching her in the chest, while yelling, I'm killing you. So, I ran upstairs to get my brother and beat on the door but he ignored me and my mom wouldn't help. So, I got a butcher's knife and was going downstairs to save her... I saw she passed out and my mom's husband told my mom if you go get her the same thing is going to happen to you and Red and Tom is coming to get her.

He said you ain't going to make it to your soulmate and he is going to die and go to hell, because he won't have you to help him pass his heaven and hell tests.

Red and Tom started on-line schools from the dream of my mom's husband from the devil with my stolen inheritance money from the 1987 911 rape call in Detroit, Michigan at one of my childhood homes.

Detroit Police told me they seen the Red and Tom movie and don't drive up North unless I got a wad of cash and a full tank of gas. Plus they said to watch out for the curse that my mom's husband put on 75 freeway that's going to cause you to run off the road through time. I came across the curse in 2014 from 1987. My Chrysler jeep almost flipped over and blew up but God's guardian Angel's drove my vehicle to the gas station by force and stopped my jeep on air.

Going back to when I was rapping Tupac, my mom's husband stood behind me and put his private on my butt and asked me do you feel uncomfortable and my little sister was in the kitchen but she didn't understand what was going on. So, as soon as I could, I got a weapon to defend myself because I knew that he would try something then he said, he was working night shift and had to go to bed, so he left me alone for the time being.

One day for my birthday, my mom yelled, honey she bumped

me, but I didn't touch her. So, my mom's husband caught a live mouse on a trap and told my mom to pick it up and put it in my face and make me stare into its eyes. He was a minister at church and she was a Bible school teacher and over the babies nursery.

My mom's husband told Red and Tom police officers that I was a baby Genius and they wanted them to make me dumb and flunk out of school, the Red and Tom police officers asked my mom's husband, what did I do to him? He said, nothing, he's just evil and inject me with AIDS and HIV and give me a slow death.

In 1982, my mom told me that she was getting married to the guy who ended up being the founder of

Red and Tom Police Officers organization. I was 5 years old, and I broke out crying uncontrollably and I sensed evil. My mom said if you don't want me to get married I won't do it. I said okay, then she got married to him on Wednesday night Bible class in a transition, which isn't good supernaturally. Doing things in a transition, destroys blessings and I knew that at 5 years old but the Pastor should've known that he was evil and he didn't belong in our family, nor our church. This is also their heaven and hell tests and they all failed.

God's Angel's explain to me that if the devil spiritually attacked you and stole your gifts to see and connect soulmates, left your other ministry do the job to marry connected soulmates that they can see and spiritually identify that they belong until God heals you and takes you to heaven and restores your heavenly gifts.

I am writing this book to give justice to my victims in my family and 911 of Red and Tom Police Officers and Attorney Generals.

The Mayor of Detroit, Michigan in the 80's, even secretly faked his death, to fight Red and Tom Police Officer's members and Attorney Generals underground and he had several members of the Federal government helping. He fought until he got severely sick, and died in 1987. He tried to stop the Red and Tom movie and 911.

No matter where I was at, the first African American Mayor of the City of Detroit, Michigan and his sister always found me and without tracking devices. They could see me through time and through heaven. They had spiritual connections from God himself.

One day, that Muslim Red and Tom member said he got jumped by the OES and Mason's but he doesn't know which branch. He said he was choked by chains, set on fire and beat. He said he thought that he was going to die. He said they got the apartment manager too and they was told don't mess with Jennifer or else we will be back to finish the job. However, when I saw him, no burn marks but he was so scared he begged me not to be late to my meeting because he didn't want them to think that Red and Tom did something...

He said it happened through time, I said that ain't no evidence. No crime committed and you a Red and Tom member plus OES and Mason's would be heroes.

The State of Michigan's Social Workers came to my high school and got me out of class and asked about the recording and evidence. I went to Northwestern high school in Detroit, Michigan, 1994. I wore a hidden recording device at 15 years old for the State of Michigan, to catch the founder of human trafficking through sexual assault on a State female Worker, and she wanted child abuse evidence to also prosecute him. If I had gotten caught, he would've tried to get me killed, raped, human trafficked.

In 2015, it was reported that the gay Muslim died that was a Red and Tom member, he lived in New Center Plaza Apartments and he helped blocked the children's keys to heaven from being copyrighted and published and caused it to be auctioned with other Red and Tom members including devils Angel's and the devil himself.

Going back to when I was at Central Michigan University, a Caucasian girl in her twenties told me that she will teach me everything from the Red and Tom movie and she will take me to a Red and Tom police officer and he will give me those kids. Then she said, "I give up, I can't do this, and left."

Just so you lawmakers know that God wants foster care kids' college education paid at 100% because they are left to defend for themselves without family.

Going back to when I was 8 years old, a Detroit Police lady Officer asked her partner that why he didn't he take me out of the house before witnessing my mom's husband witchcraft? Now, they can't afford to take me out, afraid that I will show other kids and risk their safety. However, they didn't know that I was an ordained Angel from God and I had an Angel with 70% of God's power to help me fight evil. Me and the Mayor of the City of Detroit, Michigan was a Supernatural force and team and we fought against evil with Detroit Police in the 80's to the 90's with his sister, who was a marriage counselor.

Later on in 2014, that Attorney at Team Wellness refused to file my claim to get my government benefits so I could pay for storage and when I was attacked by a stranger on the street behind my back with mace at a cross walk, an ambulance worker called Lincoln Park Police and they locked me in a psych ward on my way to pay my storage bill. However, if the Attorney got my benefits approved, in 2014, I could've put the bill on auto pay and saved the children's keys to heaven, now after 10 plus years it could be anywhere. It's called Mu'men 'Elleyyeen.

Now, he could've contacted Red and Tom members because he had their names to get a payoff, that's probably why he ignored me and blocked me from help.

If one should find several Red and Tom members missing, God sent his Angel's and opened up a portal from heaven and the Angel's killed them and put them in a super body bag and threw them in hell for eternal life.

My mom's husband slapped my sister, while she was pregnant,

busted her lip, while me and my siblings were away. If I saw that I would've sprayed raid in his eyes and knocked him out with a casts iron skillet in the head and called 911 to arrests him for attacking a pregnant girl and an unborn child. That's 20 years in prison...to life.

God had soldiers fighting to save the Pentagon from being crashed into by a plane by 9-11 victims, many 1st responders who were killed, who are now God's Angel's that tried to save lives and saved lives during 9-11 and regular citizens. Innocent souls of the heavenly kingdom were attacked and killed and all victims deserve and will get justice from heaven, it's God's rules.

Now, my mom says do what the Bible say and no shacking, if you love God follow his commandments... So when I ask her about all the abuse, she says she doesn't remember and her now deceased ex-husband, only hit me once. However my therapist and psychiatrists discovered over a decade of physical and sexual abuse through treatment and memory. They are trained to retrieve information from cold cases of any abuse, human trafficking, murder i.e., and they know if you are telling the truth or not through treatment.

Going to my former Air Force Veteran, therapist before she physically assaulted me at Team Wellness located in Eastern Market, Detroit, Michigan, and I pressed charges on her, she said that my brain hid years of abuse, murder, rape, human trafficking to protect me and that's why I forgot until they helped me recover my memory through treatment, plus the power of God through the Mayor of the City of Detroit as my Angel through listening to his machine heartbeat.

Now, don't forget to get my ordained written book by God, called God Alone Five Keys to Heaven, to learn how to connect to your loved ones and that was killed and in 9-11 as your Angels for comforting from God.

Even if you get a sign from God that your loved ones made it into heaven, you will have comfort and can rest.

This goes for any victims from explosions, bombings, massacres killings i.e.

I became the Oracle in 2015 in the hospital, by beating the Oracle at her own game. All Red and Tom members started coming through the walls invisible, recognizing me.

Then they discharged me from the hospital and let me go.

My mom's husband recruited my used-to-be high school friend on Wreford St. in Detroit, Michigan, to start a fight with me and get me suspended from several basketball games. I went feral, and fought her, her cousin, a teacher, and a crowd and blindly hit a police, but they dropped the charges when they realized the teacher put my hands behind my back and let a 300lbs girl hit me and I beat his ass. Then the police took us to the mini police station and separated us and I hit her in the head with my mind and when she came to attack me, I ran up on the wall and kicked her. Then the Detroit police told me to leave and they told me the lights went out and she was flipped backwards into the air so they closed off the room, because no one was near her and they had no evidence of the attack. I was told that I had to go to 36th district court before a Judge and explain myself, then the Detroit Police got a call and said the Judge changed her mind and said, self-defense.

I was blocked from Harvard basketball team recruiters and my dream to go there to study law was robbed.

The Principal said that her GPA was too low and she never should've been in Northwestern high school and she picked a fight with someone else so they expelled her permanently.

Those people that bought my storage E-019 at Public Storage with the children keys to heaven must be Red and Tom members, because if they weren't they would've returned that book because it is linked to fight against human trafficking against kids, rape, child abduction, murder i.e.

It's been a decade and no book and this is proof, Public Storage got a record of who has this book.

My mom's church members sold her and her husband the house that used to be owned by the doctor 100 years ago from the Red and Tom movie. My mom's husband asked the church members can you hear screams outside the home and the husband answered no. This question alone, should've made him turn down the sale and rethink their decision to sale them this house. Instead, they sold them the home and housed human trafficking, child rape, 911 plans, stealing childrens' virginity, beatings, stealing inheritance, a home for dirty cops and Attorney Generals i.e. Then the husband noticed a damaged bedroom door on my brother's bedroom and it was from my mom's husband trying to knock it down to kill him, but he said the kids did it and the church member who was the husband and deacon of the church, believed him and didn't call the police.

Now, the Police Officer that told my mom's husband that I should arrest you, but I respect you was Detroit Police for stealing childrens' virginity of two of my sisters. The Detroit Police asked him how did it feel, you lucky man. I was 8 years old witnessing this...

My Angel's said not selling them that house was a heaven and hell tests for their keys to heaven and they failed.

They should've sold the house to someone else with peaceful spirits and not asking about screams.

My Angels heard the recordings of the conversation through heaven and heard everything and this is why everyone is charged.

Red and Tom means break security because it's Police doing the crimes.

Now, Red and Tom Police Officers asked my mom's husband at 8 years old can they rape and molest me and he said no because my daughter Mu'meen goes through time killing dirty cops and devil Angel's and he is scared of her because she works for God from heaven.

Now, had my two sisters told about their virginitys being stolen when those two Detroit Police reports Angels asked, arrests would've been made and prison sentences would've been given and Red and Tom Police Officer's and Attorney Generals organizations wouldn't been created. Also, God would've taken both of them to heaven and restored their entire bodies, and healed their brains to protect them from being destroyed mentally, because God did this for me in God Alone Five Keys to heaven, book.

Now that it's clear that stealing virginity incident isn't my sisters' fault, they were helpless kids in Middle School and blindsided and over powered. I witnessed the whole thing and I was threatened with my virginity being stolen at 8 years old if I didn't clean my room, me and my other sister.

Going to August 18th, 2024 in the afternoon at Kroger in Lincoln Park, Michigan on Dix & Southfield Rd. at self-checkout. While I was documenting 9-11 as a witness, this devil's angel had a disturbed look on her face and when I noticed she said excuse me very rudely. I moved, but she had an attitude. Then she said you didn't move over enough, now if I hit your ass then you'll move. Then I told her, then you'll get your ass beat. I didn't hear you. You think I'm going to let you put your hands on me... Then Kroger's employee and customers said to me, that you're in the right and it's her fault. Now, Kroger's cameras recorded this entire incident and when she threatened me. She was African American, around 5ft 7inches, 170lbs.

At Central Michigan University, in Mt. Pleasant, Michigan in my two sorority sisters apartment in 1996, the phone rung and I yelled, don't answer it, because it sounded like it was coming from the forces of hell. They said anyways and my mom's husband came through the phone as a script, which is a clone through witchcraft and he threatened to kill everybody. So, I got a butcher's knife and yelled, I'm not scared of you, and he said you're the only one not scared, I'm going to leave you alone and he left.

Then my other sorority sister that was studying journalism called my soulmate dad the Mayor of the City of Detroit, Michigan and he beat everybody's ass that gave my mom's husband the address to where I was at, stole my collector's coins, got credit cards in my name and buried Red and Tom members.

The storage being auctioned is from the dream and Red and Tom movie that the devil gave my mom's husband and from the Red and Tom's Police Officers movie that they produced with an empty storage with videos of the childrens' keys to heaven.

Attorney, R. M. V., who's law firm was in Bingham Farms, Michigan, EEOC vs Burger King in Mt. Pleasant. Attorney, R.M.V., name was made up by my mom's husband in 1987 and changed on a birthday certificate to look German. He was given my inheritance money to open up a law firm to go against EEOC and represent Burger King in Mt. Pleasant, Michigan. The Judge in Bay City, Michigan was paid off too with my inheritance money, sent through Red and Tom Police Officers from my mom's husband, and to make the jury an all-white racists group if gone to trial. The judge and Burger King's Attorney said how about that drink after the Bay City, Michigan Judge helped Burger King win the discrimination case. The judge said let's go out to celebrate the winnings and the Burger King's Attorney Agreed.

The EEOC was wrongly charged $60,000 and when I got a hold of one their Attorney's to tell her, she didn't listen, and in 2015 I came to her office working as Chief of Staff for the recent City of Detroit, Michigan Mayor and she wouldn't talk to me. I went to her website and it says she fights crime and hates evil, so she should've opened her door to me to solve this cold case that's connected to 911 planning in 1987, human trafficking, child rape, i.e.

The EEOC, Detroit, Michigan office is owed $60,000 from

burger king in Mt. Pleasant Owner. From August 31st, 1999...

For solving this 37 years old cold case that also includes the 9-11 plans to destroy the World Trade Center, back in 1987, I want to honorary badge and membership from every government agency in the world for solving this case because it's goes through international waters through forensic audits and especially in America and Canada. Now, I also earned several heavenly kingdom Angel's from God, to assist me with retrieving information from the Red and Tom's Police Officers, Attorney Generals, i.e. organization that was established back in 1987 that derived and was funded, from my stolen inheritance from a 911 rape call, that included the Thomas sisters share of the money from my full blooded siblings.

Now, don't get me wrong, the Chief of staff tried to help me when she worked as an Attorney for the EEOC but the court case was fixed and linked to Red and Tom Police Officers and Attorney Generals organization from 1987 in 1999. The judge ruined her reputation in a law newspaper for lawyers but when I fought for the keys to heaven, I could've gotten her respect back for her with my Angels and I. We fought the devil and his Angels ourselves. See God Alone Five Keys to Heaven, book as proof.

Now that the Bible that my mom's husband gave my sister to read that wiped her memories, was a Red and Tom Bible and not King James Version Bible.

My mom's husband paid Red and Tom Police Officer's print and to put a ton of Red and Tom Bible's into churches. So, if kids got molested, raped human trafficked, sold and has no memory in all denominations, this is where it all derived from — a dream from the devil himself that he put in my mom's husband's head. He gave me one at 12 years old and I threw that shit in the trash. If you have these Red and Tom Bibles, burn them.

My mom's husband told me I had a twin and Red and Tom Police Officer's told me that I was stolen out of the hospital at birth. Later on in my twenties on Seward St., in New Center Plaza

Apartments, a gay Muslim showed me the Red and Tom movie baby abduction and he said it was me. So he said go to the Fisher building on W. Grand Blvd in Detroit, Michigan and go meet your twin. She was supernatural, sitting in a chair, moving my arms and she connected her soul to my soul. She was me through time but from the pasts. I figured it out.

It was like a supernatural clone.

When Red and Tom Police Officers recruited two Central Michigan University male students to stalk me and my dorm room, one Caucasian and one mixed, a Mason on Detroit Police Department took me took the Police immediately gun range and shot up a shooting target posters head, chest, and balls with a 9mm and told me to put the poster on my front dorm room door and this would scare anyone. Then he gave me a 357 and a rifle to shoot but the 357 blew me back, but I blew off the head of the poster and the gun range manager said that I know how to handle myself with firearms.

My mom's husband said, now I know what to do with this house, now I know what to do with America and the world through Red and Tom Police Officers organization and Attorney Generals.

The suburban Red and Tom Police asked my mom's husband, if y'all got that much money, how come y'all don't live in a mansion, why are y'all in a ghetto? He said because a black man in a mansion, in a white neighborhood would bring attention. It's easier to do it in the ghetto, where no one notices.

Now, at 15 years old I opened a Comerica Bank account and the branch manager found my inheritance but said I was too young to get it. At 18 years old my inheritance disappeared and I don't know what Comerica bank did. Around or about 2010 bank of America's branch manager in New Center in Detroit, Michigan found my inheritance but she said I had to remember my pin number or else it goes back to the Federal government. We'll my inheritance was stolen on a 911 rape call in 1987, and I was 8 years old, so who put my inheritance in Comerica bank and bank of America by pin number because I was a child. The Federal government has to give it back regardless of a pin number, because an 8 year old can't have a bank account. I barely got approved at 15 years old.

One of Red and Tom Police Officers wives came to the house to talk to my mom, because my mom's husband told the Red and Tom Police Officers to do the same thing to their wives and kids that he did to me and my siblings as initiation and steal their virginity's with their wives approval and or by force.

If the wife doesn't, slap her... One Red and Tom Police Officer said that his wife will kill him and or his daughter won't ever talk to him again.

It is November 2nd, 2024 at 5:24 A.M. means the 24th hour, and Angel, Mayor, C.A.Y, of the City of Detroit, Michigan, and the first African American Mayor's birthday and time. He also spiritually willed me his other Angel Harry, who is God's right hand Angel, and I received and was assigned Angel Harry from God himself after I earned all of the childrens' keys to heaven book called Mu'men E'lleyyeen for every child in the Universe and forever and also after I earned the keys to heaven book called God Alone Five Keys to Heaven, for every adult in the entire Universe and forever. Angel, Mayor, C.A.Y., fought for my life and inheritance plus safety and the keys to heaven till death in 1997. As soon as he connected within God's supernatural heavenly kingdom system to find me as a toddler and throughout my life, he knew that I had belonged to his lifeline because spiritually ordained us as heavenly kingdom Angels and we had the same supernatural powers as well as forces that connects from God through God's entire heavenly kingdom to help us throughout the entire Universe and forever. Angel, Mayor, C.A.Y, knew that the devil himself has stolen me as his supernatural Angel seed from God in heaven, before he had become the devil and got kicked out of heaven, while trying to take God's place as the only God, and the devil manipulated many other heavenly kingdom Angel's to abort God's heaven and join evil forces with him in hell in his new kingdom and fight eternity against any souls that believes in God and Jesus and any heavenly kingdom Angel's and heavenly kingdom members. This is where the devil, himself, placed me well into many eras into time of the future, where I couldn't create a heavenly kingdom Angel ordained lifeline with Jesus himself as my ordained soulmate. I knew that Jesus was my soulmate at 19 years old, which is the Quranic code from the mathematical equation in the Quran proves God's signature and heavenly kingdom's miracles. The devil falsely connected me to his devil's angel that later robbed me and I found out that he is a Red and Tom's Police Officers organization's member from 1987 through a 911 rape call, where Red and Tom's Police Officers organization was founded to bomb the World Trade Center and the Pentagon, i.e..

In 1987, when I was 8 years old, just about to turn 9, several Red and Tom's Police Officers organization's members asked my mom's husband, who is the founder of Red and Tom's Police Officers organization, he they could rape and molest me... These Police Officers were Dearborn, Michigan Police Department Officers, Lincoln Park, Michigan Police Department Officers, Eastpointe, Michigan Police Department Officers. They also agreed to falsely arrests me on false criminal charges from the devils dream and create false criminal records, including falsely arrests Erskine Lee Reed in the future on false charges because the devil knew that God ordained him to later become his right hand Angel, and a right hand Angel to his Angel Harry and my right hand Angel, and the devil wanted Erskine Lee Reed as his personal devil's right hand Angel but he refused because he doesn't hurt children, so he sacrificed himself for God and the entire heavenly kingdom. These Red and Tom's Police Officers organization's, i.e. members said that through the devils dream that they are going to send me to Stonecrest Hospital under Psychiatric Care and assign me to Dr. John Head and then send me to Team Wellness to continue mental health care under Dr. John Head, Psychiatrist, where he was to have injected in my blood stream Haldol, where it could cause heart arrhythmia, including brain damage, stroke symptoms, loss of balance, loss of focus, i.e. even end up on life support or even death and Licensed, Clinical Therapist, Dorothy Robinson, Air Force Veteran, where she was to get to know me and act like she was there to help, press charges on all suspects involved in the child abuse crimes plus stolen inheritance, i.e., then after 5 years, she was to begin physically assaulting me, while trying to provoke me and have me falsely arrested, while all along she was told to provide all therapy notes, to Red and Tom's Police Officers, organizations, i.e. members, so that they know if I got my memory back and was no longer with amnesia. The Licensed Clinical Therapist, Dorothy Robinson, Air Force Veteran, even got Team Wellness Lawyer involved and he acted like he was going to have all of the Red and Tom's Police Officers, i.e. organization members prosecuted, instead he contacted them, to steal my inheritance and joined forces, and helped the founder of the Red and Tom's Police Officers, organization members get away, and live comfortably in a private condominium downtown Detroit, Michigan secured gated community and he had originally planned the bombing of the World Trade Center, bombings as well as the Pentagon, he was the founder of human trafficking, child rape, taking children's virginity's, abduction, murder, and terriosm, i.e. This is why the devil had his Red and Tom's Police Officers, i.e. organization members put me into the mental health hospitals, including Henry Ford Hospitals throughout the State of Michigan and on from there so I can't mentally be a witness to the devils dream and against their 37 year hit and orchestrated attacks on me and everywhere that I go through my government information, and illegally evicted from my own properties where my inheritance was used to purchase from the 1987 911 rape call, and the Red and Tom's Police Officers organization members, paid the State of Michigan Judges and all Lawyers involved in any legal process, or earned benefits even from me working that they would be denied and my inheritance was invested within the State of Michigan and throughout the American government system including Canada, the Queen of England, properties and Real Estate, and throughout the world. Red and Tom's Police Officers organizations, i.e. members made personal oaths to the devil himself to complete his entire dream, including block my future, success, College degrees, Careers, i.e. and take everything that I own and should own into the future. Red and Tom's Police Officers, i.e., organizations took my inheritance and purchased railroad companies, Public Storage and later charged me monthly rent and then illegal auctioned my storage unit E-019, at 3650 Enterprise Dr., Allen Park, Michigan 48101.

Insurance companies, Auto & Life, Professional Driving companies that has contracts with the railroad. Now the devil told his Red and Tom's Police Officers, i.e., organization's members that everyone, government entity, College, educational institutions, Corporations, Healthcare industry, i.e., has to agree to carry out the devils dream, if they take my World Times Future inheritance money from my collector's coins from the year of 1010. The devil himself had his Red and Tom's Police Officers, organization members take my inheritance to Hollywood and produced his devil's dream movie that showed the future of the World Trade Center, bombings that was planned in 1987 from a 911 rape call. In this devils dream, he was planting amnesia into my brain cells so that I could forget the planned attacks of the future, and every time that I would end up at a devil's Angel Red and Tom's Police Officers, i.e. organization members territory, I wouldn't remember and they could keep harming me and or killing everyone around me and if I remember, the devils plans, take my life. Now, at 8 years old, as soon as I heard the devils evil plans, the these evil Red and Tom's Police Officers, i.e. organization's members, at 8 years old God sent me Angel, Mayor, C.A.Y., of the City of Detroit, Michigan, World War II Army Veteran and Air Force Pilot, he told me the Lord's Prayer forwards because my mom's husband taught me the Lord's Prayer backwards, so that I couldn't connect to God in heaven and get help. Angel, Mayor, C.A.Y., City of Detroit, Michigan World War II Army Veteran and Air Force Pilot showed me the Lord's Prayer and how to communicate with him through my mind, and he said to me that if any time that I needed his help, to say the Lord's Prayer and he'll show up and help me. So I did just that, my mom's husband threatened me and I said the Lord's

Prayer one morning at 5 A.M., at 8 years old, and Angel, Mayor, C.A.Y, showed up to me providing his heavenly kingdom Angel's services. From this point, I was able to build up supernatural powers and forces directly from Jesus and God himself and I used those supernatural powers and forces to protect my siblings from child rape, abduction, murder, as well as all the children in the Universe, including against terrorism and fighting to prevent the bombing attacks against the World Trade Center and the Pentagon, i.e. Plus supernaturally fighting against the devils dream and his evil plans during the present and for the future. Now, at 12 years old, I remembered Army Veteran, D., J., F., telling me that he was going to make me his girlfriend and I yelled and screamed at him saying, "NO, I'M NOT." Then God sent him out the house running down the street yelling in pain. Then in 2012 of February, in a Victorian home, in Dearborn, Michigan with rented single rooms, Retired Veteran Army Veteran, D., J., F., was in a single rented room, one room away from me and the devil himself took me hostage, and said to me, if I don't go in his room that he was going to throw me in front of a bus. Now, in 2015 from August 16th, 2015 through August 25th, 2024, I started to remember the devil's dream, that he placed in all of his devils Angel's minds that are Red and Tom's Police Officers, i.e., organization's members, but Henry Ford Hospital Psychiatric Ward, licensed Nurses, put memory loss medications in my blood stream and made me forget and this is why presently in 2024, with God's help, I am remembering and Henry Ford Hospital's are the devil himself Red and Tom's Police Officers, i.e., organization's members hospitals, and they agreed to orchestrate the devils dream attacks on me, when accepting my inheritance, from my collector's silver coins from the year of 1010 and this was planned back in the year of 1987, on a 911 rape call in Detroit, Michigan at one of my childhood in residence in zone 8.

Now, because these false arrests were preplanned in 1987 for the future on a 911 rape call when I was 8 years old, those false arrests are now kidnappings, abductions, held in hostage situations through the government system, through the State of

Michigan Police Department Officers, with badges, and fully loaded guns. This means that The State of Michigan Police Department Officers kidnapped, and abducted me with a loaded gun and handcuffs and placed threat on my life, if I didn't follow their devil's Angel's commands, and they've committed statutory rape on me as a child and threatened me with future arrests when becoming and adult, and making life and death threats on my future child, while robbing my inheritance from my silver collector's coins from 1010, and forcefully exchanging my life, as well as future with them and their generations, kids, grandkids, wives, i.e. Moreover, a few times during my appointment with Dr. J., H., Psychiatrist at Team Wellness, at 2925 Russell St., Detroit, Michigan 48207, the Staff told me that Dr. J., H., has to bury both of his adult children and just the other night on October 31, 2024 at the Universal Soul Circus, in Detroit, Michigan, God himself showed up in the supernatural spirit through his heavenly kingdom. Anointing forces and explained all of the attacks on my life and everyone involved plus on the heavenly kingdom Angel's. God told me that he not only took Dr. John Head, Psychiatrist adult children for prescribed injection medication that hospitalized me by emergency ambulance and could've placed me on life support and killed me, God took the life of Retired Army Veteran, D. J. F. daughter after he falsely dialed 911 and lied on me and got me locked up and got my entire life stolen in my storage since my childhood including God's miracle for children in the entire Universe and forever, plus falsely enslaving me for 10 plus years through Lincoln Park, Michigan Police Department Officers and through the enforcement of the Judge, the Prosecutor, and the Jail Officers. Including false imprisonment in Henry Ford Wyandotte Psychiatric Hospital Ward Hospital in Wyandotte, Michigan. God explained to me when Retired Army Veteran, D., J., F, falsely failed 911 on me, that placed him inside of my childhood residence, when I was a child, threatening to make me his girlfriend and as a Red and Tom's Police Officers, i.e., member, he was given my inheritance from my silver collector's coins from the year of 1010, and back from a 911 rape call in 1987.

It is November 2nd, 2024 at 7:40 A.M., means vision, for anyone, soul corporate representatives, government representatives, and any business deals on behalf of my entire heavenly kingdom, there is no legally taking any rites of passage, heavenly kingdom earned miracles, gifts nor profits, without paying sacrifices from Alpha and Omega, especially from when my son Jesus was killed by the Jewish people and pierced to death, from the crown of his head to his feet. Every prophet, every heavenly kingdom Angel and every heavenly kingdom member and since my son Jesus's era in B.C., had to pay sacrifices and pass all of their heaven and hell tests to earn every heavenly kingdom miracle, keys to heaven and Angel's wings, plus the power to heal, i.e. How dare you think, that any one of you, and your companies, including government officials, i.e., think that you don't have to pay sacrifices to me as the only God in the entire heavenly kingdom and throughout the entire Universe plus to my son Jesus himself. There isn't no writing any contractual legal agreements, under any State nor any government that can over power my supernatural ordained heavenly kingdom rules, that's been in existence since the beginning of time before Adam and Eve. These supernatural forces will automatically become in effect on everyone's lifelines and no one can't start, nor stop it but myself God or either my son Jesus, and as well in transition because my Angel, Jennifer DiAnne Thomas, Queen of heaven, key holder of every soul in the entire Universe and forever and the only one to assign my heavenly kingdom Angel's to every soul throughout the entire Universe and forever, and as my son's Jesus soulmate and wife of my entire heavenly kingdom, she will soon possess those same exact powers, because she was born as well as anointed to bare the other half of my son's Jesus cross and as the only eternal God, she has done a supernatural, miracle job since a toddler. Amen... So, if anyone start valuing themselves and or there business services or connections or anything over my entire heavenly kingdom, which includes my heavenly kingdom Angel's and heavenly kingdom members, my signature, my Angel's picture, i.e., and you can't earn the actual physical images and documentation plus spiritual connections to me as the only God, nor can you afford my presence because you don't possess any heavenly kingdom credits nor as a child, you will get annihilated, and evicted from life and as the only God, I will show you your exact worth and your business services worth down to hell for eternal life while burning in rage for robbing my heavenly kingdom and by sending the violators in hell, this is how all of the heavenly kingdom powers and forces, gets burned off of the devil's angels and returned back to my entire heavenly kingdom by force.

Going back to the house on Linwood, i.e. my mom's parents, her best friend from church, the Mayor, and told him to give me my inheritance from the year of 1010, silver collector's coins to the Queen of England, and he said he ain't giving her shit. Then my mom's husband said, he will have his police officer's get it to her, and or the United States of America, Red and Tom's members through their government jobs, as well as Attorney General's. So, one day at 12 years old, I was watching the news and all of a sudden, the media introduced the Queen of England, and said she must be rich, look how rich she is... She had a gold horse carriage, a royalty rob, a diamond crown, soldiers in expensive uniforms with riffles and a huge parade. Then it was a man next door that argued with my mom.

Then and pushed her down, So, I went to get a butcher's knife then he explained to me why and we immediately shook hands and made up and he told me that I could be his daughter, and he was looking for me since birth and he never told anyone and he was the Mayor, of the City of Detroit, Michigan. I also remember talking to him on the phone at even 8 years old, when I was attending Woodward Elementary School, formerly in Detroit, Michigan on Wreford St., and my mom's husband told him that he can't talk to me anymore, because I was getting too smart, because when he said, y'all got the same gene's, I told him DNA, and he said that I thought you were going to say a pair of jeans that one wears. Then my mom's husband said, "if you were a man, you've would've claimed her on her birth certificate." "I claimed all of my kids." This conversation is over...

So, we me and my siblings plus my mom, and her husband went

to a church on the Eastside near Cadieux Rd., and Morang Rd., and across from Baskin Robbins and 7 Eleven in 1991. When I went into the church's basement, I overheard the Pastor of the church, and my mom's husband talking saying whatever you've gotten us signed up with these Red and Tom's, i.e., Police Officer's end it, because they are harassing our church member's. Then my mom's husband said, "You told me you needed help with church bills and I helped you and now it's a problem. So, the church contacted my Angel, soulmate dad, Mayor, City of Detroit, Michigan, World War II, Army veteran... got the Mayor involved, and the Detroit, Michigan Police, to stop harassment. Red and Tom's Police Officer's told, from the Red and Tom's video, if the church and or any victims and on future generations lifelines, don't perform sexual acts on their members, so the next day, my mom's husband, told two of my siblings to come in his bedroom, and he showed them a torture video if they didn't do sexual acts, and then my mom, busted in the room and told them to leave. That's when I went into the basement and said a prayer and performed a ritual to stop evil and it worked so good for 3 weeks, that my mom's husband couldn't sell them in the basement to police officer's and friend's, nor do human trafficking. Then one of my sister's told on me to my mom's husband who was a victim of losing her virginity and being sold in human trafficking, when I thought it was mental illness and sick. I thought if I am helping you, to stop evil. Why would you tell on me? So, my mom's husband threatened me, because he said that no one could go into the basement anymore. I stopped several police departments and Attorney General's from doing evil, including internet terrorists from doing evil including human trafficking at 12 years old, they was pissed because they couldn't triple their stolen investments from a 911 rape call, so, they put a hit on me, and my future plans, and places to live, work, i.e.

The devil has lost supernatural powers by robing heaven when he transitioned into the devil himself and recruited other Angel's and transitioned them as devil's angel's, so they lost the heavenly kingdom's ordained power God, and those three headed dog's that guards the gates of the devil's kingdom, is their eye and seeing and supernatural hearing dogs, to locate any heavenly kingdom's supernatural elevations and to get around the entire Universe, so they are all disabled, and handicapped, and Jesus, A.K.A., Yeshua, Isa, states in his ordained original bible, that the blind lead the blind end up in a ditch. This is who the devil himself, got to make personal oaths, to join his evil devil's kingdom. The blind, deaf, and dumb...with infinity curses by God almighty his self. I figured out the devil's evil hell eternal life system at 12 years old.

Put God's signature here

www.ingramcontent.com/pod-product-compliance
Lightning Source LLC
Chambersburg PA
CBHW061421300426
44114CB00015B/2016